# Vajournal

## Isabella BUNNELL

# Hello.

This IS VAJOURNAL! A book EXPLORING What IT Means TO be A feminist, Woman and ALL Round boss-AS BITCH. Vajournal is an ILLUSTRATED Collection of pages INTENDED to AMUSE, educate & FACILITATE your EXPRESSION of feminist IDEAS and HAPPENINGS with WORDS and PICTURES. Think YOUR boobs look FUNNY? Draw THEM! Got Catcalled TODAY? EXPLORE how THIS makes YOU FEEL!

With PAGES for you TO Write down your Emotions and spaces FOR YOUR own drawings AND DOODLES. VAJOURNAL is your ally in your FIGHT against THE patriarchy and your companion on THE Road To SELF-ACTUALISATION OK, Maybe not THAT, But it WILL HELP you Explore your THOUGHTS and FEELINGS you Beautiful Feminist.

WRITE in it
DRAW in it
EXPLORE with it

VAJOURNAL FOREVER!

THE idea
THAT WOMEN's bodies
CAN be Catagorised &
COMPARED TO Fruit
& objects ONLY leads
TO THE objectification
OF the Female FORM.
IT'S time TO Stop
comparing WOMEN'S
Bodies to
FRUIT

Write DOWN and DRAW how you FEEL ABOUT your BODY

WHAT are THE best
and WORST things
ANYONE has ever
SAID about IT?

Write DOWN and DRAW your thoughts ABOUT the BODIES of THREE people close TO you:

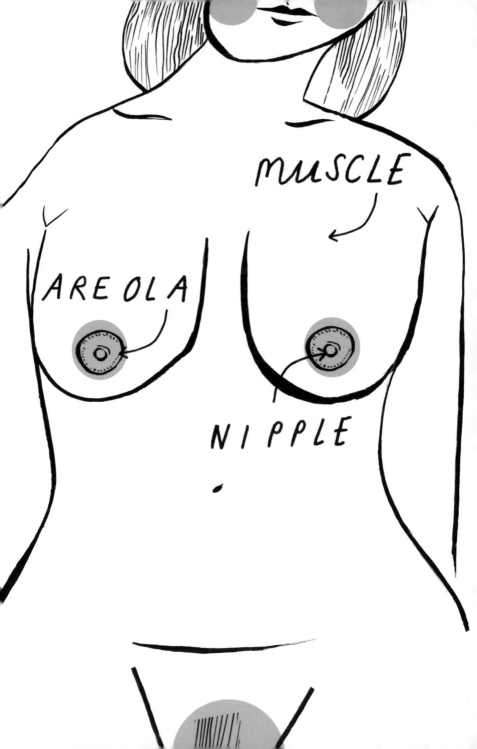

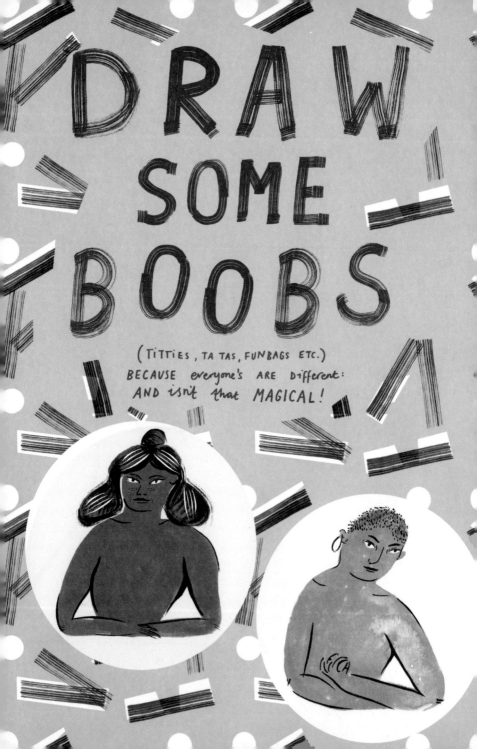

# DRAW *your* OWN boobs

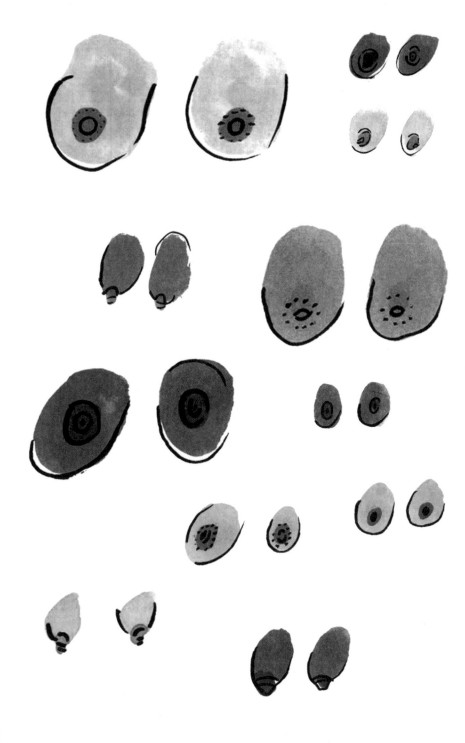

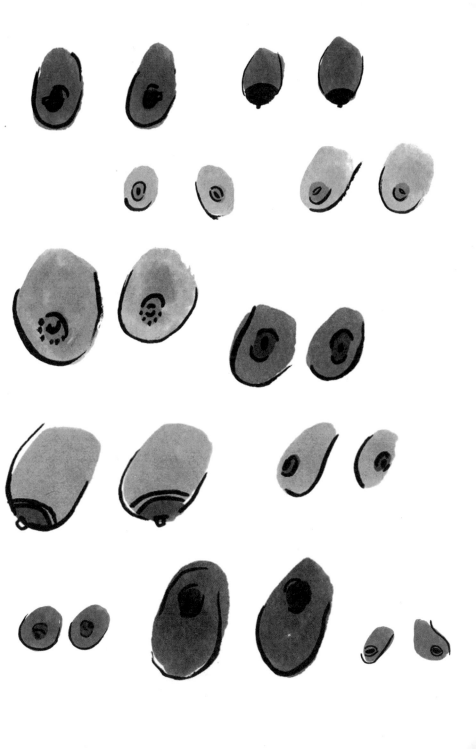

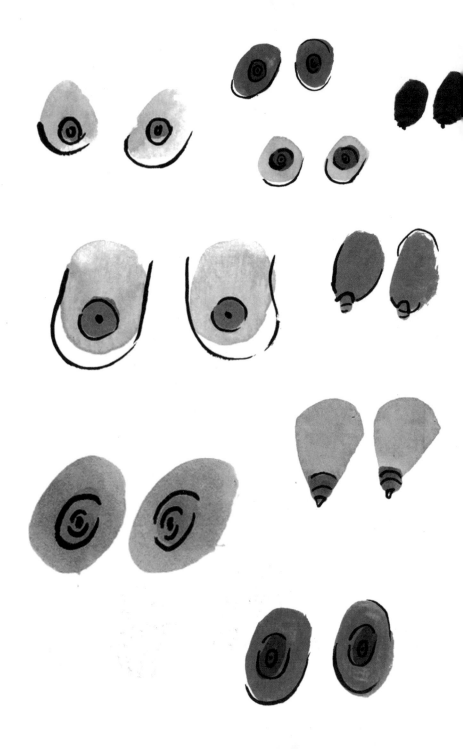

The airbrushed media ideal of the woman's body is
so unrealistic and yet so omnipresent that we can't help compare
ourselves and find ourselves wanting.

Design an alternative magazine.
What do you think women want to hear about?

TO LOSE CONFIDENCE IN ONE'S BODY IS TO LOSE CONFIDENCE IN ONESELF

—SIMONE de Beauvoir

# KNOW YOUR BIKINI STYLES

FULL BRAZILIAN

POSTAGE STAMP

Heart ATTACK

LANDING STRIP

## BUT DO WHATEVER (YOU) WANT

BRAZILIAN STRIP

STRING

MARTINI GLASS

BRAZILIAN TRIANGLE

AU NATUREL

TRIANGLE

DRAW your BIKINI line

# THINK of an OUTLANDISH new STYLE

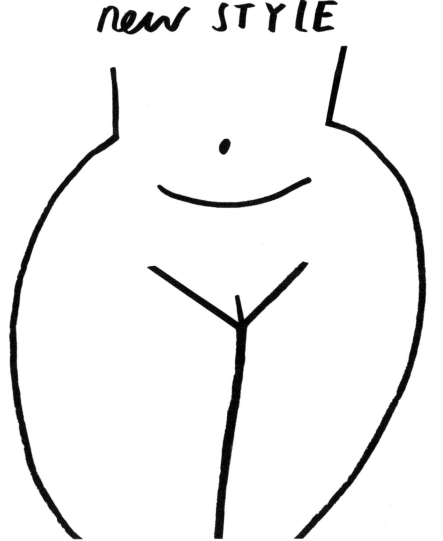

# Vagina Owners Manual

# LE VAGINA

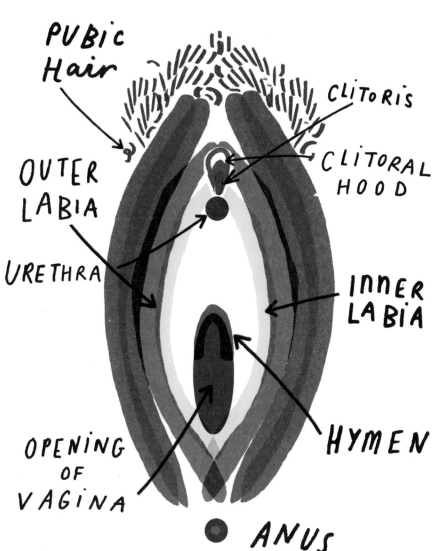

PUBIC Hair

CLITORIS

CLITORAL HOOD

OUTER LABIA

URETHRA

INNER LABIA

HYMEN

OPENING OF VAGINA

ANUS

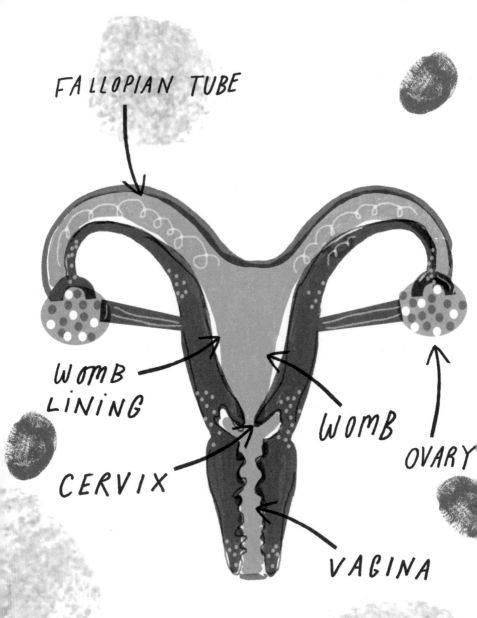

FALLOPIAN TUBE

WOMB LINING

CERVIX

WOMB

OVARY

VAGINA

# ON the Blob

Despite the fact that every woman in the world experiences menstruation, there is a culture of silence and shame around it. Assumptions are made about emotional imbalances and ads show turquoise liquids being cryptically poured onto sanitary towels.

It's time to end the stigmas and silence!

## THERE WILL BE BLOOD!
### (GET OVER IT)

# Talk about IT

How regular is your period? How long does it last for?
What does it feel like? Do you have sex whilst on your period?

When SHE bleeds
the SMELLS
I know change
COLOUR.
There is IRON in
HER Soul, on
THOSE days
SHE smells
LIKE a
GUN.

Jeanette Winterson

# Follicular Phase

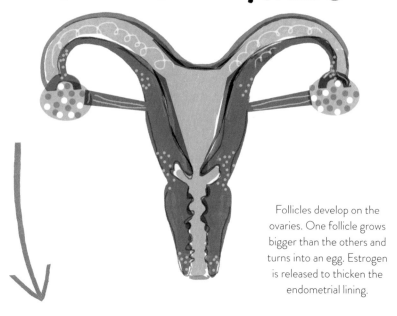

Follicles develop on the ovaries. One follicle grows bigger than the others and turns into an egg. Estrogen is released to thicken the endometrial lining.

# Ovulation

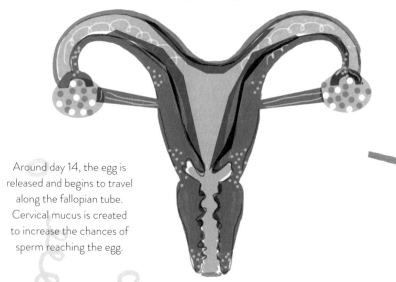

Around day 14, the egg is released and begins to travel along the fallopian tube. Cervical mucus is created to increase the chances of sperm reaching the egg.

# Menstruation

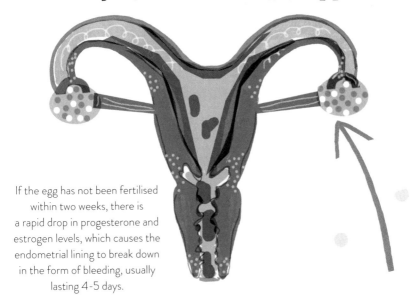

If the egg has not been fertilised within two weeks, there is a rapid drop in progesterone and estrogen levels, which causes the endometrial lining to break down in the form of bleeding, usually lasting 4-5 days.

# Luteal Phase

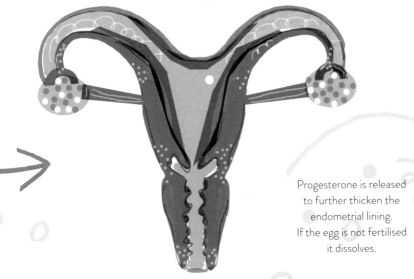

Progesterone is released to further thicken the endometrial lining. If the egg is not fertilised it dissolves.

# PERIOD *facts*

Studies have found that empathy levels increase during the follicular stage of the cycle.

During the luteal phase you will expend 2.5-11% more energy. Women often eat 10% more during this phase as progesterone causes the body to store more fat and protein.

The average western woman menstruates around 450 times in her life. Prehistoric women only menstruated 50 times, and women in developing agrarian cultures menstruate around 150 times.

The human female egg is the largest cell in the human body. It is the only human cell that can be seen with the naked eye.

A modern woman uses up to 11,000 tampons and spends on average £20,000 on sanitary products throughout her lifetime.

In the UK a 5% tax was introduced on tampons, whilst men's disposable razors remain untaxed.

If you had £20,000 to burn what would you spend it on?

# CHART *your* CYCLE

Highlight the day of your last period
and how long it lasted.
Do this for a couple of months to
work out your average cycle,
and then mark when your periods
are due for the rest of the year.

## January

| | | | | | | |
|---|---|---|---|---|---|---|
| 1 | 2 | 3 | 4 | 5 | 6 | 7 |
| 8 | 9 | 10 | 11 | 12 | 13 | 14 |
| 15 | 16 | 17 | 18 | 19 | 20 | 21 |
| 22 | 23 | 24 | 25 | 26 | 27 | 28 |
| 30 | 31 | | | | | |

## February

| | | | | | | |
|---|---|---|---|---|---|---|
| 1 | 2 | 3 | 4 | 5 | 6 | 7 |
| 8 | 9 | 10 | 11 | 12 | 13 | 14 |
| 15 | 16 | 17 | 18 | 19 | 20 | 21 |
| 22 | 23 | 24 | 25 | 26 | 27 | 28 |

## March

| | | | | | | |
|---|---|---|---|---|---|---|
| 1 | 2 | 3 | 4 | 5 | 6 | 7 |
| 8 | 9 | 10 | 11 | 12 | 13 | 14 |
| 15 | 16 | 17 | 18 | 19 | 20 | 21 |
| 22 | 23 | 24 | 25 | 26 | 27 | 28 |
| 30 | 31 | | | | | |

## April

| | | | | | | |
|---|---|---|---|---|---|---|
| 1 | 2 | 3 | 4 | 5 | 6 | 7 |
| 8 | 9 | 10 | 11 | 12 | 13 | 14 |
| 15 | 16 | 17 | 18 | 19 | 20 | 21 |
| 22 | 23 | 24 | 25 | 26 | 27 | 28 |
| 30 | | | | | | |

## May

| | | | | | | |
|---|---|---|---|---|---|---|
| 1 | 2 | 3 | 4 | 5 | 6 | 7 |
| 8 | 9 | 10 | 11 | 12 | 13 | 14 |
| 15 | 16 | 17 | 18 | 19 | 20 | 21 |
| 22 | 23 | 24 | 25 | 26 | 27 | 28 |
| 30 | 31 | | | | | |

## June

| | | | | | | |
|---|---|---|---|---|---|---|
| 1 | 2 | 3 | 4 | 5 | 6 | 7 |
| 8 | 9 | 10 | 11 | 12 | 13 | 14 |
| 15 | 16 | 17 | 18 | 19 | 20 | 21 |
| 22 | 23 | 24 | 25 | 26 | 27 | 28 |
| 30 | | | | | | |

## July

| 1 | 2 | 3 | 4 | 5 | 6 | 7 |
|----|----|----|----|----|----|----|
| 8 | 9 | 10 | 11 | 12 | 13 | 14 |
| 15 | 16 | 17 | 18 | 19 | 20 | 21 |
| 22 | 23 | 24 | 25 | 26 | 27 | 28 |
| 30 | 31 | | | | | |

## August

| 1 | 2 | 3 | 4 | 5 | 6 | 7 |
|----|----|----|----|----|----|----|
| 8 | 9 | 10 | 11 | 12 | 13 | 14 |
| 15 | 16 | 17 | 18 | 19 | 20 | 21 |
| 22 | 23 | 24 | 25 | 26 | 27 | 28 |
| 30 | 31 | | | | | |

## September

| 1 | 2 | 3 | 4 | 5 | 6 | 7 |
|----|----|----|----|----|----|----|
| 8 | 9 | 10 | 11 | 12 | 13 | 14 |
| 15 | 16 | 17 | 18 | 19 | 20 | 21 |
| 22 | 23 | 24 | 25 | 26 | 27 | 28 |
| 30 | | | | | | |

## October

| 1 | 2 | 3 | 4 | 5 | 6 | 7 |
|----|----|----|----|----|----|----|
| 8 | 9 | 10 | 11 | 12 | 13 | 14 |
| 15 | 16 | 17 | 18 | 19 | 20 | 21 |
| 22 | 23 | 24 | 25 | 26 | 27 | 28 |
| 30 | 31 | | | | | |

## November

| 1 | 2 | 3 | 4 | 5 | 6 | 7 |
|----|----|----|----|----|----|----|
| 8 | 9 | 10 | 11 | 12 | 13 | 14 |
| 15 | 16 | 17 | 18 | 19 | 20 | 21 |
| 22 | 23 | 24 | 25 | 26 | 27 | 28 |
| 30 | | | | | | |

## December

| 1 | 2 | 3 | 4 | 5 | 6 | 7 |
|----|----|----|----|----|----|----|
| 8 | 9 | 10 | 11 | 12 | 13 | 14 |
| 15 | 16 | 17 | 18 | 19 | 20 | 21 |
| 22 | 23 | 24 | 25 | 26 | 27 | 28 |
| 30 | 31 | | | | | |

# Everyone I have EVER slept WITH

IMPLANT

The COIL

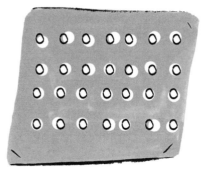

the PILL

Vaginal RING

Sponge

MORNING
AFTER
PILL

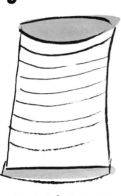

FEMALE
CONDOM

Injection

THE Patch

Diaphragm

CONDOMS

ABSTINENCE

WITHDRAWAL

SPERMICIDE

# Everyone I have EVER WANTED to Sleep WITH

# SEXUALITY

**MARK WHERE YOU**

SUPER
STRAIGHT

Mainly HETERO
with A LITTLE
HOMO

# SPECTRUM

ARE ON THE LINE:

Mainly HOMO
with A SPOT
OF HETERO

BISEXUAL

SUPER
GAY

My sexuality is not an inferior trait that needs to be chaperoned by emotionalism or morality —

ALICE BAG

# WRITE DOWN THE Anxious THOUGHTS FILLING YOUR HEAD

TAKE a
moment
TO Draw
Something
EVERYDAY
FOR 4 WEEKS

# Monday

# TUESDAY

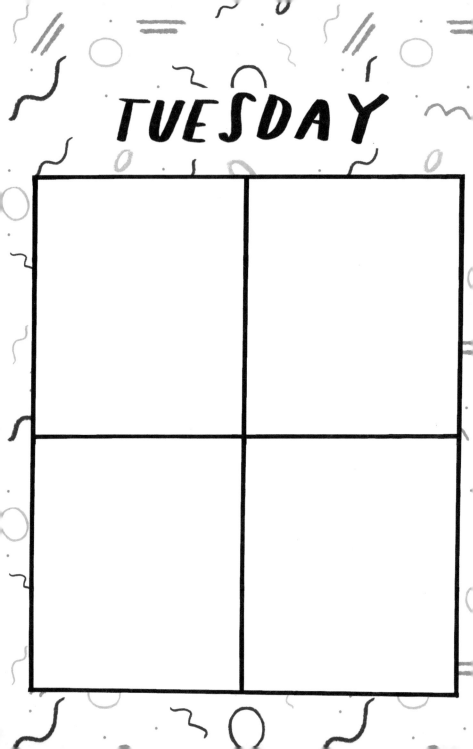

# Wednesday

# THURSDAY

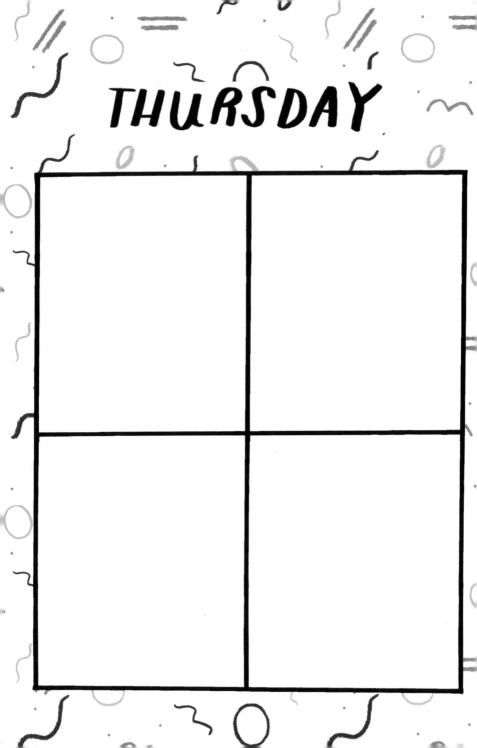

# Friday

# SATURDAY

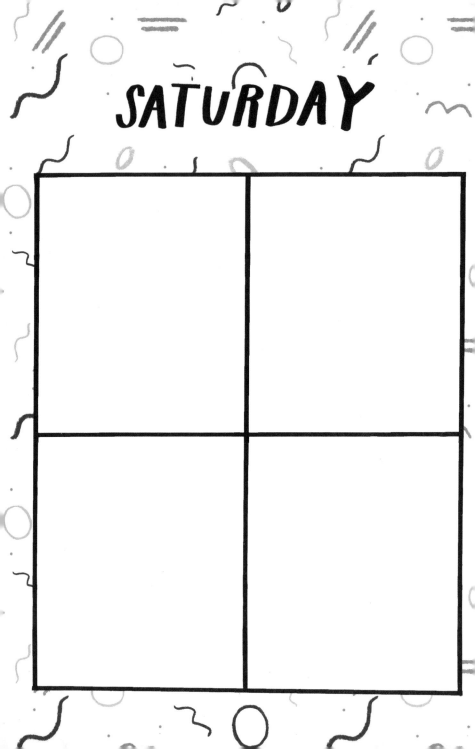

# Sunday

# JUST

# NOT

# SORRY

Women tend to apologise more for issuing instructions
or opinions, undermining themselves to appear more likeable.

Record how many times you say and write "sorry"
and "just" in a day. Try to register why you're saying sorry
and whether the apology is actually genuine.

What other WORDS DO you use TOO Frequently? DO you EVER undermine YourSELF? When? WHAT triggers IT?

When a MAN Gives HIS OPINION HE'S A Man. When a Woman GIVES Her OPINION SHE'S A Bitch

- Bette DAVIS

TURN
THE
PAGE
FOR
SOME
PUSSY

# SCARY

OF THE 2,300 WORKS OWNED BY THE NATIONAL GALLERY IN LONDON, ONLY 10 WERE PAINTED BY WOMEN

WOMEN DIRECTED JUST 5% OF THE 250 MAJOR FILMS IN 2015

TWO WOMEN ARE KILLED EVERY WEEK BY THEIR CURRENT OR FORMER PARTNER

THE DIETING INDUSTRY IS WORTH 20 BILLION PER YEAR

# STATS

THE GENDER PAYGAP STANDS
AT 18% MEASURED BY MEDIAN
GROSS HOURLY PAY

## CEO

WOMEN MAKE UP
4% OF FORTUNE
500's CEOs

WOMEN HOLD FOUR
OUT OF 22 CABINET
POSITIONS

BY THE AGE OF 13, 53% OF GIRLS
SAID THEY WERE UNHAPPY WITH
THEIR BODY

Women EARN 18%.

Less than MEN

I'M NOT
Bossy
I'm THE
BOSS

DRAW a list of your WORK goals & AMBITIONS. Where do you see yourself IN FIVE years TIME? How are YOU going TO GET there!

THE Work THAT is traditionally carried out BY Men is WHAT counts. IT defines THE Economic WORLD view. Women's Work is 'THE OTHER' Everything THAT he DOESN'T DO BUT that he is DEPENDENT ON SO HE can DO what HE does.

Katrine MARCEL

Women play a greater role in childcare and 8 out of 10 women say they do more housework than their male counterparts.

Think about your mother – how did the domestic responsibilities divvy up between her and your dad?

| MUM | DAD |
| --- | --- |
|  |  |

# GIVING NOTICE

What are THE things you silently
ACCEPT Responsibility FOR? SEE
what HAPPENS if you just
DECIDE not TO NOTICE

Pastel COLOURS and Gendered MARKETING sends clear MESSAGES which toys ARE for boys and WHICH are FOR girls. Boys get ACTION. construction and TECHNOLOGY toys. Girls GET dolls and kitchens and DOMESTIC toys. sending THE clear MESSAGE girls COOK, MEN work.

Design some TOYS you would have wanted to play with when you WERE little

# COMPLIMENTS and MICROAGGRESSIONS

- you're really BRAVE to wear THAT dress
- You're prettier IN Person
- You DON'T look like someone WHO likes FOOTBALL
- I like HOW you're NOT OBSESSED
  - with HOW you LOOK
- it's great you're so INDEPENDENT
  - You're SUCH a fun DRUNK.
- How come you're so pretty and single
- You're such a strong person

A microaggression is a backhanded compliment that is based on
assumptions and sterotypes that are ultimately degrading.

When A woman HAS SCHOLARLY INCLINATION there is Usually SOMETHING WRONG WITH Her Sexual ORGANS

FRIEDRICH NIETZCHE

She SAYS She
IS ON A Diet
AND then HELPS
herself TO
SECOND
helping
OF cheese

—NICOLAS SARKOZY ON
ANGELA MERKEL

What are the most enraging comments you've ever
heard spoken about women?

THE
BECHDEL
TEST

# ALISON BECHDEL author and CARTOONIST extraordinaire, DEVISED a test TO HIGHLIGHT gender INEQUALITY in film. DOES the PIECE in Question feature a scene IN WHICH two women talk TO each OTHER about SOMETHING other than A Man?

Write a list of all the TV shows and films you can think of.
How many pass the Bechdel test?

Draw A Scene BETWEEN a Man & A WOMAN that is IMPRINTED on your MEMORY

What is THE WOMAN Doing
IN the scene?
Why do you Remember it?

# WHO ARE your Favourite MOVIE & TV HEROINES?

The INCIDENTS that GO unwitnessed DEFINITELY help TO keep SEXISM off THE Radar AN unacknowledged PROBLEM we DON'T discuss. BUT so too do the REGULAR occurences that hide IN Plain SIGHT within a SOCIETY that HAS normalized sexism and ALLOWED it TO become so INGRAINED that WE NO longer NOTICE or OBJECT to IT. Sexism is a SOCIALLY acceptable PREDUJICE and EVERYBODY is getting IN ON the ACT.

Laura Bates EVERYDAY SEXISM

# Write DOWN your EXPERIENCES of Everyday SEXISM

# MANSPLAINING

Explaining Without regard to the fact that the explainee knows more than the explainer, often done by a man to a woman

LILY ROTHMAN of THE ATLANTIC

Write some OF your EXPERIENCES
of MANSPLAINING

WOMEN

V.S

WOMEN

When we are taught to hold our minds and bodies to unfeasibly high standards, it stands to reason that women are far more judgmental of other women than they are of men.

It takes guts and self-knowledge to battle this internalised misogyny. Register each time you think a bitchy thought about a woman you don't really know. Consider what you are criticising her for and whether you would have the same response if she were a man.

Published by Cicada Books Limited

Illustrated by Isabella Bunnell
Design by April

British Library Cataloguing-in-
Publication Data.

A CIP record for this book is available
from the British Library.
ISBN: 978-1-908714-47-3

© 2017 Cicada Books Limited

CO

Cicada Books Limited
48 Burghley Road
London NW5 1UE
E: cicadabooks@gmail.com
W: www.cicadabooks.co.uk